Wakefield

in old picture postcards

by
John Goodchild

European Library – Zaltbommel/Netherlands

GB   ISBN 90 288 4823 1 / CIP

INTRODUCTION

The years between 1880 and 1930 were for the old town of Wakefield and its surrounding villages, years of considerable change. At the national census of 1881, Wakefield's population was a little less than 31,000, at that of 1931 it was over 59,000, although these figures are not strictly comparable, as the area of the borough had itself massively increased from 1,500 acres in 1880 to over 5,000 acres, as a result of several extensions of the borough boundary — in 1895, 1900 (to include Alverthorpe), 1909 (taking in Belle Vue and Sandal), and 1921 (Lupset).

Changes in the economy of the town had occurred: the old Wakefield corn trade had almost disappeared, the cattle market was but a shadow of its former self, some once large businesses had disappeared in the post-war depression. But many of the industries in fact survived the various depressions of the period and grew: various types of factories expanded, modernised and developed new markets, those concerned with engineering and textiles mirroring such changes. The larger local collieries, some of whose men lived in the town or its suburbs, survived the depressions too, although the smaller ones ceased to be economic and pits such as the Augusta Colliery, off Dewsbury Road, with its 16 underground workers, for example, closed in 1902. A major new source of employment emerged with first the opening of Wakefield Town Hall in 1880 and the subsequent increase in the number of corporation officials, and then with the decision of the County Council of 1889 to retain its headquarters in Wakefield and the consequent opening of the County Hall in 1898. New administrative jobs were offered too in central government departments which had new branches in the town, and larger numbers were employed in industrialists' offices. By the time of the 1911 census, over 800 Wakefield residents were employed in local government. In 1888 the municipal borough, only established itself four decades earlier, became a nominal city, and in 1915, more significantly, a completely self-determining County Borough.

The town was expanding physically: the old inner areas, filled with older and often deteriorating houses (numbers of which were originally fine buildings, be it remembered) were only slum-cleared from the 1920s and then piecemeal, so that new housing was perforce located in the suburbs and beyond the industrial-cum-domestic inner suburbs of the earlier 19th century. Speculative housing schemes such as those at Plumpton Park on Westgate Common or at Belle Vue, were paralleled by the building of single houses, of semis or of short rows in various new outer suburbs of the town. The sometime lower rates of independent Sandal Magna were apparently a minor incentive to building there.

Public transport facilities were important too, as there were few private cars before 1930. The suburban railway stations at Alverthorpe, Ossett and Sandal were significant, but the horse omnibus services promoted from 1890 resulted in recognisable ribbon developments and were followed in 1904 by the more restricted routes but more frequent services of the electric trams, which survived until 1932. From 1922 the motor buses were of increasing significance, especially in serving villages which had neither tram nor convenient rail services. Wakefield remained throughout this period an important retail marketing centre, and the enhancement of cheap, regular and reliable public transport facilities greatly assisted the maintenance and growth of the town as a regional shopping centre. The new housing estates which were developed from the early 1920s, initially in fact reluctantly, were again largely in the outer suburbs, demanding yet further public transport facilities. The transport of goods by canal and inland waterway continued, even though from the end of the First World War in overall decline; the railways continued to offer improving passenger and goods opportunities, and the use of the internal combustion engine was growing from the end of the war in both numbers and significance. The period from 1880 to 1930 witnessed a vast growth in all sorts of public facilities provided by both the municipality and private enterprise: public parks, a new theatre, music halls, cinemas, a fine new water supply, a municipal electricity supply, major new public buildings, a library service, slum clearance and municipal and private housing, a

new hospital and its extension, new schools and a technical and art college, new chapels and churches, working men's clubs, modern political parties, a modern sewage works – and the list could go on.

This book contains pictorial images of but some of these aspects of change in Wakefield in the half century under consideration. The pictures themselves are from the John Goodchild Loan Collection at Wakefield Library Headquarters: naturally, numbers of aspects of local life were either never photographed or photographs of them are not represented in this collection, but an attempt has been made to illustrate as wide a range of aspects of local life as the material allows, with a particular emphasis on street scenes, where in a few instances scenes in the same street or location are shown at different periods.

At the same time, some perhaps more idiosyncratic views have also been included, together with a few in the surrounding villages and countryside, used here because some aspect of the particular picture has a direct relationship to an otherwise un-illustrated facet of the town's story. The earliest postmark on any of the picture postcards used here is 1904, but original photographic prints have been used also, the earliest of which shows the opening of the Town Hall in 1880.

S.3441   CHANTRY-ON-THE-BRIDGE, WAKEFIELD.

1. A view across Wakefield bridge from the north end. On the left, a group of children are apparently view-
ing the rebuilt Chantry Chapel, whose new front of 1847/48, built of foreign stone unable to withstand the
acidic atmosphere of industrial Wakefield, is prevented from disintegrating on to passers-by by a substantial railing. In the centre background is the White Bear, a public house stands at the point of junction of
the main roads to Doncaster and Barnsley, respectively made into toll roads in 1740 and 1758, but from
1878 and 1876 (respectively) freed from tolls.

KIRKGATE BRIDGE AND CHANTRY, WAKEFIELD

928 / 8

2. Wakefield Old Bridge. An interesting photograph, showing bridge, tramway, King's Mill, malt kiln, boat, railway grain warehouse, Aire & Calder Navigation offices, sewage outfall structure, and the rebuilt church of Saint Mary on the site of the medieval Chantry Chapel, etc.

KINGS MILL

3. The new bridge at Wakefield was opened in 1933 both to relieve the older, narrow one and to avoid the dog-leg bend on to it, shown here. This is a trade postcard issued by the cornmilling firm of Reynolds, Stott & Haslegrave, Ltd.

TOP OF WESTGATE, WAKEFIELD

4. The top of Westgate. G.F. Ziegler occupies the (unusually) stone-sided building on the extreme right of the picture, at the top of Queen Street, while behind are what appear to be numbers of Georgian buildings, although in fact in some instances they were very much older structures, modernised by the addition of new façades. Watson & Kenworthy, wholesale grocers, set up in business in 1849 and became a Limited Company in 1920: the front of their shop shown here has been rebuilt during the 1980s. On the left, the 1862 building of the Wakefield Church Institute, a pale parallel on denominational lines of the much more robust and longer lasting Mechanics' Institute, designed by A.B. Higham and built at a cost of a £2,350; it closed as a result of a resolution of its members of 1911.

Old House in Westgate, Wakefield   Valentines Series

5. William Sidebottom occupied ancient buildings in Marygate, shown here; much rebuilding occurred in this area after Corporation clearance in 1901.

6. Looking into the Bull Ring from Marygate. Motor taxis and a policeman with an interest in traffic are all now in evidence.

Westgate, Wakefield

Published by J. Ranns, Stationer, Wakefield. Valentines Series

7. The fine buildings of upper Westgate. That facing down the street was the first Wakefield Corn Exchange, built on a site acquired in 1819 and built in 1820: it was in use by 1821 but in 1825 the owner's banking firm failed and it was not until 1837 that the foundation stone of a new exchange was laid, shown here as the largest and furthest of the three buildings on the right-hand side of the street; it was opened at the beginning of 1838 and much extended in 1863/64, but the corn trade declined and in 1910 the Saloon was converted to a cinema and in 1920 the new exchange was let as a billiard hall. The Great Bull, with its two ogeetop bays which still survive, was built early in the 1770s and was certainly Wakefield's largest inn; the contents of its 50-plus bedrooms were sold in 1908 and thereafter considerable parts of the premises were used for other purposes. The fine local Wakefield & Barsley Union Bank building dates from 1879, and has carved over its main door the initials of the banking company and a representation of the head of William Stewart, the Wakefield lawyer who was its chairman.

8. A shop front: probably that of the Misses Ada and Edith Turner, confectioners, for many years at the top of Westgate.

9. A children's procession passes down Market Street, possibly en route to the park. On the left is the entrance gateway to the Victoria Brewery, by this time (from 1890) owned by the Leeds & Wakefield Breweries, while in the further distance is the Methodist Free Church's chapel of 1858, and beyond it the Post Office building opened in 1876.

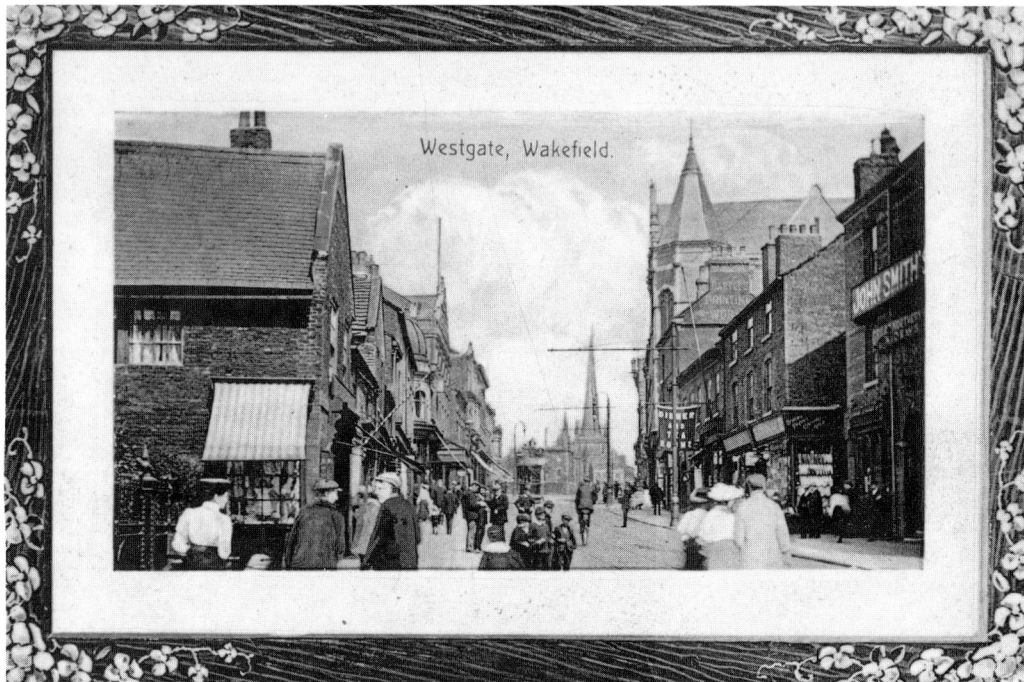

Westgate, Wakefield.

10. A view of Westgate, taken from the entrance to Westgate Chapel. The picture dates from in or before 1914 when the last trams were converted to covered tops. On the left are timber-framed buildings which survived into modern times, and on the extreme left the entrance to the house which had originally been that of the master of the Wakefield Green Coat School. On the right is the Great Northern Hotel, the building of which still survives.

11. Another top-of-Westgate view used in 1908 and showing one of the new covered top trams built in 1905, en route to Ossett. Jeremiah Dunnill's music shop is at the lower corner of Cheapside; note the fine shop windows.

WESTGATE, WAKEFIELD

12. Another view of the top of Westgate, looking into both Silver Street and Little Westgate. Not many of its buildings survive. No trams have yet appeared (1904), and numerous cabs await custom in the area anciently known as the Corn Market, from the open mart held there before the days of corn exchanges. On the right can be seen the entrance to Market Street, leading to both the Cattle Market and Denby Dale.

AIR VIEW OF WAKEFIELD CATHEDRAL 16287

13. Four aerial views of Wakefield in the 1920s. Two of this series are from photographs taken on 14th July 1926, and the others are probably also of that date. The pictures well illustrate the appearance of the town and two of its inner suburban areas, before piecemeal destruction had taken place, and the ancient pattern of the town was destroyed.

Central Wakefield looking north.

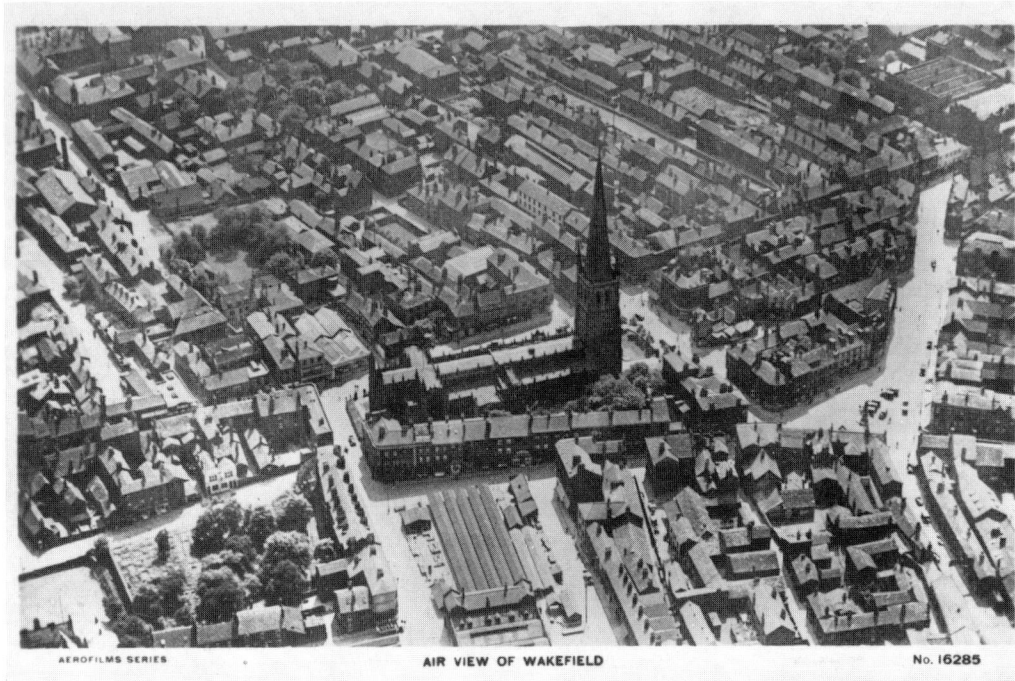

14. Central Wakefield, looking south.

AEROFILMS SERIES — AIR VIEW OF WAKEFIELD, SHOWING RIVER AND FACTORIES — No. 16286

15. Wakefield Bridge and the Calder Vale Road area.

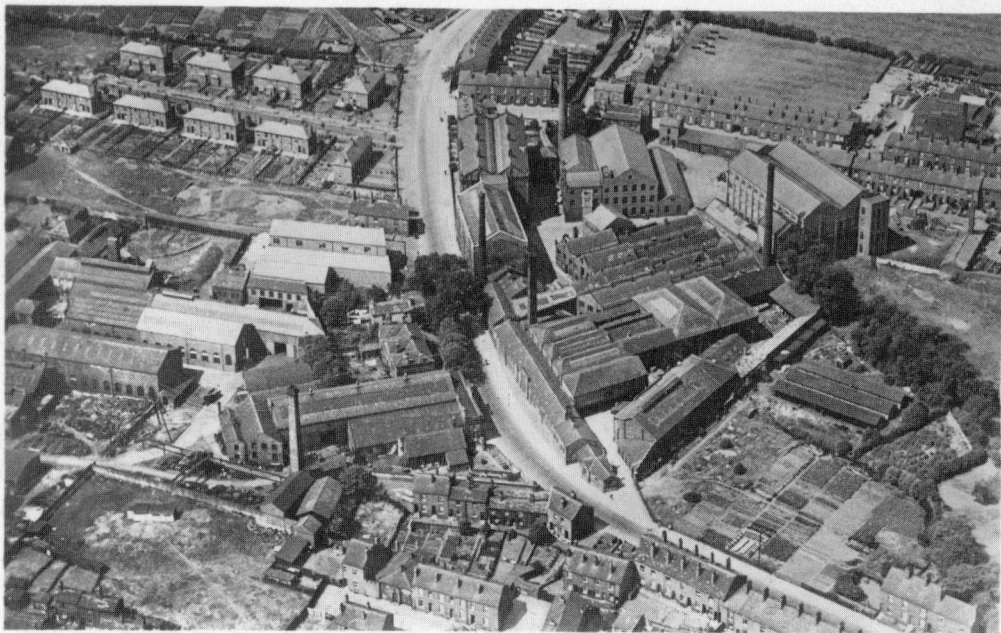

AIR VIEW OF WAKEFIELD, SHOWING ALVERTHORPE ROAD DISTRICT

16. Alverthorpe Road, Henry Street and Farne Avenue.

WAKEFIELD, WESTGATE. Aug. Bank Holiday 1922.

17. A wet Bank Holiday! At the beginning of August in 1922, heavy rain led to this situation of modest flooding. On the left is the multangular lodge to Plumpton House, and beyond it the speculative housing of the rows of Plumpton. The Westgate Station clock can be seen in the distance, with the swollen beck in the centre and on the right the tram track with its central poles. The three-storied House of Recovery building at the end of Lawefield Lane can be identified, together with the yard which formed Marriott's Buildings.

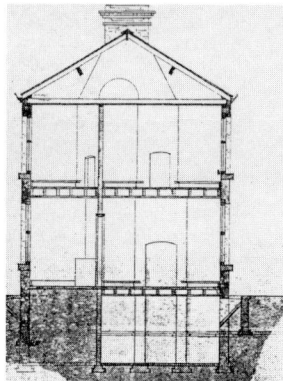

18. The corner shop: William Clark's Carlton Street Provision Stores were at number 27 Carlton Street, at its junction with Lawefield Lane, and were established by Clark in the 1890s to serve the newly-developed working class area of New Brighton, comprising Carlton, Gaskell and Brighton Streets. Designs for houses in Carlton Street were drawn up by the Wakefield architect William Watson: he had established his practice in Wakefield in 1864, and was responsible for the design of many local buildings, including schools, hospitals, churches, chapels and mills, as well as for designing housing developments.

19. The Market Place, which had its name changed to the Bull Ring in about 1910, was cleared of the group of buildings which filled its centre, and which included the Boy & Barrel Inn, in 1898, while the electric tramway was opened in 1904: the photograph is thus between these dates. The ancient centre of the town, the Market Place, consisted of several areas for the sale of various products: a pig market, flesh booths, fish shambles, fruit market, cow market and bull ring. The market was removed from the town streets under the powers granted by the Market Company Act of 1847.

20. The Boy & Barrel Inn stood in the middle of the Market Place, in the midst of areas used for the sale of particular commodities. The block of buildings included the medieval Toll Booth or Town Hall, but part of the block was demolished in 1857 and the larger part of it, including the buildings shown here, in 1898.

21. The Market Place − still using its old name on a card posted in 1908 − and with cabs still horse-drawn. On the left is the entrance to Union Street, on the right the entrance to Westmorland Street and lower Northgate.

22. Boots were one of the first large national firms to establish a branch in Wakefield, and they had premises which opened into both the Bull Ring and Cross Square. These young ladies were obviously shop workers of the post-First World War period.

23. Another Market Place view, posted in 1920, although showing a much earlier situation. Since the turn of the century shops at the corner of Westmorland Street had changed occupiers from H.J. Robinson to Bradley's, Rose & Co had become Boots', John Ellis's had become J.C. Kaye, grocer, whilst next to him in both cases were Legards, the leather merchants.

24. Wakefield Cathedral about 1900. The fabric of the church had been recased from the late 1850s and beginning with the tower and spire, being completed with the south porch (1881) and the south wall (1886). The Act to create a new diocese was passed in 1878 and the first bishop, William Walsham How, was installed in 1888. This picture is probably taken from an upper floor of the premises of G. & J. Hall, the Wakefield photographers established in about 1849; on the left are the premises of Abraham Grace & Sons, carvers, gilders, paper hangers, picture framers, etc, and in the 1790s the premises of one of Wakefield's earliest banks, that of John & William Shackleton, grocers and bankers. On the right the sign probably marks the shop of Grace & Firth, woollen merchants; nearby was the Lord Rodney Inn, which lost its licence in 1908 as redundant. In the background are some of the houses built in the new Westmorland Street (named after a local solicitor and director of the Market Co.), which were rebuilt from the 1850s.

25. Cross Square with on the left the Grand Clothing Hall of 1906 and on the right the Black Rock − which only became an inn in the later 19th century − and M.I. Eggleston's beyond that, with Webster's café and shop. The buildings which had almost closed the lower part of the street, and created the square, had been cleared away in about 1909, while the market cross which provided the other part of the name, had been demolished in 1866. This card was used in 1920.

26. Almshouse Lane, with the almshouses of Cotton and William Horne on the left, looking towards Upper Kirkgate. The almshouse buildings date from a rebuilding of 1793, but almshouses for ten poor women were endowed by Cotton Horne in 1647 and for ten poor men by his son William in 1669. The 1793 rebuilding provided for almshouses each for two poor persons, together with one for a nurse. Negotiations for further rebuilding began in the 1890s and in 1901 they were rebuilt in Cotton and Horne Streets. On the right hand side of this setted street are the Wakefield Old Baths, built by a company established in 1873, the foundation stone laid in 1874 and the premises purchased by the Corporation in 1884 for £2,200.

27. The Springs in the '90s. On the right, the wall of the Old Vicarage garden, from 1880 the Conservative Club, and adjoining it, the Wakefield Waver, and pinfold behind. The Waver was the public watering place of the town, and medieval references are made to it. This view was drawn and engraved by W.H. Milnes, junior, in 1890, and published in a series of etchings of the town.

IN KIRKGATE, WAKEFIELD

28. Shops and ancient buildings in Kirkgate, at the entrance to Beaumont's Yard and just below the entrance to the present Sun Lane. The picture typifies the very varied appearances of even the main streets of the town, with houses and shops with different numbers of stories, some ancient timber-framed, some more modern, some with newer fronts on older buildings.

29. Kirkgate, looking up from the end of Legh Street. The variety of the forms of the frontages of the buildings is most marked; few of these buildings survive today.

30. Pincheon Street, Kirkgate; the rather grand entrance to The Sultan Lodging House of James Charlesworth — by now Mrs. Charlesworth's lodging house at numbers 4 and 6; the Charlesworths also ran the lodging house in George Street, next to the then Baptist Chapel.

31. The Six Chimneys and the Crown & Anchor in Kirkgate. Alfred Lund of the Crown & Anchor appears in the register of electors of September 1903, but not in that of the previous year, while the picture shows no tramtracks − the tramway system was opened in 1904. The building of the public house had been rebuilt in 1816, and references occur to its being to let in 1832 and to an inquest being held there in 1840. The Six Chimneys was a much more ancient building, with the date 1566 carved in two places upon it. The earliest known document which refers to it is dated 1688, and alludes to the structure as the Six Chimneys. It may have been built by one of the Wakefield branch of the Savile family, as their badge of an owl was carved upon one of the timbers. The building collapsed in 1941. Behind the house rises the chimney of the Anchor Foundry, the site for which was leased in 1839, and the buildings of which were demolished at the end of 1963. The Anchor Foundry lay off Legh Street, which derived its name from the landowner G.J. Legh.

32. The Butcher's Arms Yard at Eastmoor carries the name of the yard, and above it an advertisement for good stabling. The Butcher's Arms still stands on the west side of Stanley Road at Eastmoor. Note the break in the brickwork at the rightside of the arch, indicating differing building periods.

33. Lawefield Cottage, in Lawefield Lane, before the lowering of the park wall, the widening of the road and its extension through to Horbury Road. The cottage, in the midst of luxuriant gardens, is shown on the enclosure map of circa 1794, although it may then have been a comparatively modern building, as it does not seem to exhibit the steepness of pitch characteristic of earlier, thatched roofs.

34. Denby Dale Road. A pleasant, tree-lined artery, created as part of a virgin route from Wakefield to Manchester, built as the Wakefield and Denby Dale Turnpike or toll road, under an Act of 1825. It was not until the 1890s that housing infilling occurred, and the public park on the left of the picture was created. On the extreme right can be seen part of the boundary wall of Thornes Church, itself built in 1829-1831.

35. The Bishop Blaize Inn at Thornes ('dedicated' to the patron saint of woolcombers, a trade carried on in Thornes village), dated from at least the earliest 18th century. The adjoining railway was opened to traffic in 1840, and beyond one of its bridges can be seen the remains of Thornes pump, built in 1827 above a public well, in part to provide water for horses using the newly-built Wakefield and Denby Dale turnpike or toll road. The Bishop Blaize was demolished in connection with the quadrupling of the adjoining (by then LMS) line, the work on which was done in 1926.

VIEW FROM WAKEFIELD PARK, WAKEFIELD.

36. Wakefield from Lawe Hill. An interesting view, with the first bandstand on the extreme left and the point of crossing of the West Riding & Grimsby and Lancashire & Yorkshire railways a little to its right. Mills, malt kilns and corn warehouses of Calder Valley and the riverside area can be seen quite plainly, together with, in the foreground, the new houses and almshouses on and off Denby Dale Road. The card was used in 1915.

37. Roofs from the Town Hall tower, looking towards the Cathedral. In the foreground are buildings in Wood Street, in the left centre the buildings in the Bull Ring which survive; that in front of them is the Boy & Barrel block which was demolished in 1898. The chimney is almost certainly that of E.P. Shaw's soda water manufactory.

38. Providence Street, Northgate, and the yards which branched off it were demolished under a Wakefield Corporation Compulsory Purchase Order of April 1934.

39. Providence Street presents today a completely different appearance to that shown in this photograph. The street was developed from the 1790s and in 1801 reference is made to a 'New Street called Providence'. The streets and the yards which branched from it, were demolished under a Wakefield Corporation Compulsory Purchase Order of April 1934.

40. Library Yard derives its name from the Wakefield (subscription) Library which was established in 1786: for some time the library was located in premises at the Northgate end of the street. The growth of the yard is illustrated from the number of tenants shown in the deeds: 1725 four, 1787 six, 1795 nine. In 1826 it was described as 'a fine spacious and open Yard'.

41. Library Yard, Northgate, was demolished under a Wakefield Corporation Compulsory Purchase Order of April 1934.

42. Gills Yard, off Northgate, was only slum-cleared in the 1950s. This is a view looking along the length of the yard, with the building of the Albert Memorial extension of the Clayton Hospital in the background, as raised by one storey in more modern times.

Wentworth Terrace, Wakefield.

43. Wentworth Terrace, very much tree-lined, looking towards Northgate and with St. Austin's Roman Catholic Church on the right; the card was posted in 1928.

Sandal Road, Wakefield.

44. The road from Wakefield to Barnsley had been turnpiked under the Act of 1758, and for many years thereafter Wakefield and Sandal had been quite different communities, separated by a mile or so of open country. But population growth had led to the erection of new houses at a distance from the town. Here, one looks towards Haddingley Hill and Wakefield, with Providence Terrace in the middle distance, a long terrace of back-to-back houses facing Manygates Park. The tramline runs on the far side of the road, and was not doubled at this point until 1924.

45. Doncaster Road, Belle Vue, with the entrance to Fall Ing Foundry (of 1787) on the left, newly-built shops − with homes above − on the immediate left, and somewhat older two-storied buildings beyond, with the three-storied Quaker Meeting of 1772 beyond them and its graveyard beyond it. On the right is the wall and surmounting rail of the cemetery of 1859, and behind that part of the Belle Vue speculative housing development, and in the distance St. Catherine's Church, opened in 1876.

SANDAL STATION LANE

46. Agbrigg Road from the railway overbridge. The West Riding & Grimsby Railway was opened in 1866 and the railway station at a similar period. Only two of the villas shown here existed in 1890, when the area was mapped by the Ordnance Survey.

HEATH COMMON, WAKEFIELD.

47. The Jolly Sailor at Heath Common derives its dedication from the adjoining Barnsley Canal, which was opened, from Wakefield to Barnsley in 1799. This picture shows the inn as part of a group of agricultural buildings, and long before rebuilding into its present form. Behind the line of the canal rises the Wakefield Golf Club house, which served the golfcourse on Heath Common itself, and which had been erected in 1897.

48. The Borough Market Hall and new Market Place. The Market Company was established by an Act of 1847, and the streets there and around it were laid out on the Rectory House estate for the purposes of the new market, being named after members and officers of the new Company. The Market Hall was built in 1851, with John Child as contractor, and the market was opened to the public on 29 August 1851. On the left of the picture is Smallpage Yard, which still exists in part, in the centre distance can be seen the Roman Catholic Schools, and to the right the cheap-book printing works of William Nicholson & Sons, built in 1871. The Market Company was bought out by the Corporation in 1902.

49. Newmillerdam derives its name from the new mill on the dam which was apparently constructed originally by 1285 and possibly in 1280, although re-located and rebuilt in later times, while the area of the dam was much enlarged and its surroundings beautified as part of a gentleman's estate. The mill shown here was probably rebuilt by 1830, and corn grinding was itself continued there as late as 1960.

50. Built as a supplementary mill to the watermill at the end of Netherton Lane, Coxley or Sandy Lane Windmill was built (from map evidence) between 1810 and 1813. The windmill in nearby Middlestown was also described in 1813 as 'recently erected'. An earlier, wooden windmill in Horbury, on the opposite side of the Calder, had been built in about 1756 and was demolished in about 1792.

51. From about 1890 until Nationalisation in 1947, the administrative headquarters of the great West Riding coalmining firm of J. & J. Charlesworth, Ltd, were at Milnes House in Westgate. Their collieries stretched from the banks of the Aire of those of the Don, and for several decades they were the Coal Kings of the West Riding coalfield. This photograph, prepared in connection with an early motor car accident law case, shows the railway crossing at Robin Hood near Wakefield, with Charlesworth's colliery dimly in the background.

52. The countryside around Wakefield provided few sites able to power waterwheels which could turn textile machinery, and in consequence considerable numbers of steam engines were introduced in the 1780s and (particularly) the '90s to power wool-preparing, spinning and cloth-fulling machinery. However, here in Coxley Valley the stream was dammed and a waterwheel-powered mill opened in the later 1780s – probably 1787. Two rows of cottages were erected, one with top-storey weaving shops, and the mill ultimately adopted steam-power. A major fire in December 1926 destroyed the mill, although a part of the premises continued in use and is still used today. The photograph shows blanket tenters, on which the finished blankets after fulling were put to dry.

53. The aqueduct at Stanley Ferry is a scheduled Ancient Monument. Built to carry an improved line of the Aire & Calder Navigation to Wakefield, replacing that used since about 1702 which had almost entirely followed the circuitous course of the Calder, its first pile was driven in July 1836, the foundations completed and the first stones laid in May 1837 (west side) and May 1838, and the whole opened on 8 August 1839. It was a stupendous work, a suspension aqueduct, and contained 760 tons of iron, with a draught for passing vessels of 7′6″. It remained the sole means of the Navigation crossing the Calder until a parallel, modern aqueduct was opened in 1982.

54. The Barnsley Canal's entrance lock at Heath remained in use until early in the 1950s. Although the canal was opened from Wakefield to Barnsley in 1799, this section was built on a new site in 1816, to replace the early use of the bed of the adjoining stream, where a surviving stone arch still shows tow-rope cuts. This view shows the tollhouse and lockkeeper's cottage, some of the stabling, and, on the right, some cock boats, drawn by boats coming up to Wakefield, but left here for passing up the canal.

55. Walton (no. 11) lock, the penultimate lock on the flight leading from the Calder to the Level leading to and beyond Barnsley. The upper lockkeeper's cottage is on the left. The Barnsley Canal had been opened here in 1799, but the locks below Barnsley were all lengthed from 58 to 79ft in 1881.

COPYRIGHT W&D's

BAR HOUSE, HEATH, WAKEFIELD

LILYWHITE LTD.
ALL BRITISH PHOTO PRINTERS

56. Agbrigg Bar on the Wakefield and Weeland turnpike or toll road. The route from Wakefield via Pontefract and Knottingley to Weeland near Snaith − Weeland was the point to which normal tides flowed on the River Aire, and below which was a free river navigation − was financed as a toll road under an Act of 1741 and was only disturnpiked in 1878. At Crofton, this road was joined by the turnpike to Doncaster, the Redhouse and Crofton, and the portion between Wakefield and Crofton was transferred to the latter's body of trustees under an Act of 1862. This tollhouse dates from probably the beginning of the 19th century, and was somewhat similar in design to that at Newton Bar. A modern house on the site today still commemorates in its name the old toll bar here. The rise in the road in the distance is occasioned by the Barnsley Canal passing below it at this point.

The Ford
Horbury Junction

57. At Calder Grove, a branch of the Wakefield & Denby Dale turnpike road ran down to the Calder, from whence an ancient ford connected with Horbury. In the background, a weir crosses the river, and just to the right of centre stands Horbury Mill, an ancient corn and cloth-fulling mill which was one of the three compulsory corn grinding mills in Wakefield and its vicinity until the abolition of the Soke custom in 1853. Millfield Lane still commemorates the existence of the mill, some of whose walls are still to be found.

58. The turnpike road tollbar at Bar Lane, near the top of Stanley Hill. An entirely new road between Wakefield and Aberford had been authorised by special Act of Parliament of 1789, and it was completed in sections over the ensuing few years; tolls continued to be charged until the road was disturnpiked in 1882. Tolls had been charged on all the main roads meeting at Wakefield, and two roads − Denby Dale and Ings roads − had been built specifically as toll roads. The Austerlands (via Huddersfield) and Aberford roads both ceased to be toll-maintained in 1882, and were the last in the vicinity of Wakefield to possess tollbars.

59. A country lane, thought to be near Chapelthorpe. In some ways a typical view of a country lane or even of a major turnpike road. The road surface was frequently made of broken limestone, brought in partly from the quarries near Skipton, while the overall width of even major roads was only about 30 feet. A foot and horse way of thick stone slabs — a causey of causey stones — was almost always laid down alongside a road from at least the earlier 18th century, and one is shown in this photograph on the left. Strict regulations enabled local highway surveyors to enforce the cutting of the hedges which adjoined public highways.

60. A three-horse omnibus at Outwood, on the Wakefield to Lofthouse horse 'bus service. The Wakefield City and District Omnibus Co Ltd. was promoted in 1890, after long discussion of such a project, and by 1891 it was operating services from Wakefield to Lofthouse, Alverthorpe, Agbrigg, Thornes and St. Michael's (Westgate End). By 1898 these services were somewhat changed: Alverthorpe — which of course had a station — had no service, that to Thornes was extended to Calder Grove, one ran to Sandal and Newmillerdam and one to Horbury. The company was hard hit by the coming of electric tramways in 1904, although it had considered promoting tramways itself, and in 1905 it went into liquidation.

61. Early in 1922, experimental bus services were introduced by the Yorkshire (West Riding) Tramways, the company which ran the Wakefield area tram services, and the subsidiary company, West Riding Automobile Co Ltd., was formed in 1923, while a new bus garage had been opened at the end of 1922 at Belle Isle. In the 1920s, among many other new bus services, this route from Wakefield via Walton and New Crofton to Newstead was opened by the West Riding, and here Leonard Gill stands with his conductor in 1929.

M.Brearley.
P.O. Lake Lock.

Aberford Rd.

62. Aberford Road at Stanley, with the cinema, opened in 1920, on the left. The card was used in 1928, when its sender comments: 'Busy Road, Cars' galore. Traffic over 1500 per day, all sorts.'

63. The main road between Wakefield and Austerlands (on the county boundary near Saddleworth) via Horbury and Huddersfield was turnpiked under an Act of 1759. Horbury Bridge was of course much older, standing on a natural rib of rock which had more anciently been a fording point. The bridge collapsed in May 1918.

64. Wakefield Bridge from the weir end. On the left are the King's Mills; until 1853 the mills possessed extensive compulsory corn and malt grinding rights. The buildings shown here were erected from 1872 at an estimated cost of £7,505, and were now worked by both water and steam power. The mill was demolished to make way for the building of the New Bridge at Wakefield, opened in 1933, and the last cargo of corn came to the King's Mills in September 1931. The bridge was itself constructed from 1342 and was twice widened, in 1758 and 1797: the differing styles of the widenings enable them to be still clearly seen. Behind the bridge are to be seen various industrial buildings, including distant views of buildings on the Stennard Island, and possibly of surviving houses on the Island known as Naboth's Vineyard.

65. The Cattle Market was established in 1765, when the Governors of the Wakefield Charities and Grammar School acquired the site by exchange. During the 19th century the Cattle Market became the largest in the north of England, and considerable extensions were made to the site; although the importation of foreign dead meat increasingly rivalled the Cattle Market's prosperity, and the pig market was ordered to be closed, in the 1890s the tolls still brought in £1,400 a year, and it was not until 1963 that the Market closed finally. It had been sold in 1938 to Wakefield Corporation for £9,000, when it was described by the President of the Meat Traders' Association as being 'in a sorry state'. A weekly (as opposed to the earlier fortnightly) Cattle Market was introduced in 1858, and a decade later 360,000 sheep, 50,000 cattle and 66,000 pigs were penned in the year, and large importations were made from both Scotland and Ireland. In 1904 iron pens replaced the earlier wooden ones. In the background is the home of the Carter family, owners of the adjoining Victoria Brewery: the house was later (as here) a public house, and also a lodging house. One of the Smyth Street (opened 1848) malt kilns is on the left of the picture.

66. James Brown of Wakefield was a self-made brass-founder who died in 1911, aged 63. Part of his extensive family subsequently lived en famille at number 6 South Parade, where they were variously interested in photography, painting, motoring. Here is HL 782 outside the family home.

67. A motor cycle event outside the Graziers Hotel, Market Street. The Graziers − and of course it was graziers who fattened-up cattle for the nearby Cattle Market − first appears in the trade directories in the mid-1840s; and J.H. Marchant was its landlord from 1907 or 1908 (according to the registers of electors) until the time of the First World War. This photograph boasts signs of the Wakefield Road Cycling Club, founded 1904, and of the National Cyclists Union. The junction of highways is beautifully setted.

68. A suburban railway station: Alverthorpe. The line through Alverthorpe had been opened from Wrenthorpe South Junction in 1862 to Flushdyke, in 1864 to Ossett and Batley, in 1874 to Dewsbury, when the whole of the line was doubled. Alverthorpe Station first appears in Bradshaw in October 1872; and was closed in 1964. The siding shown here ran off into a small goods and coal yard.

69. The road arch of the fine Midland Railway's viaduct at Horbury Bridge, opened in 1905, has the Bingley Arms (named after a local land owning family) framed within it. A new route, with easier gradients and bends, and still known as the New Road, was opened by the Wakefield & Austerlands turnpike road trustees in about 1830, avoiding the earlier route coming in from the right via Sandy Lane: the old and newer toll bar houses are shown.

70. At the Agbrigg terminus of the electric tramway system from Agbrigg through Wakefield to Ossett, which had been opened in 1904. The first thirty tramcars were typical examples of their period and were ordered in October 1903 and were delivered in June of 1904, coming by rail to Kirkgate station, from whence a temporary track was laid from the goods yard to the permanent trackway in Kirkgate. All thirty cars remained open-topped until 1911, and all had been fitted with top covers by early in 1914. The tram drivers tried to keep warm in bitterly cold weather by having hot potatoes in their coat pockets. J.W. Smith, the furrier at the top of Westgate, took limited liability in 1911.

71. The tram terminus at Sandal, on the line between Sandal, Wakefield and Thwaite Gate (Leeds), opened in 1904. Car number 66 was one of six built in 1906 at Preston in Lancashire; in 1912/13 the group of six cars were fitted with top covers, and it will be noticed that the car behind number 66 has such a cover. On the right of this picture is an entrance gateway, appararently to Cleevethorpe, one of the new Sandal mansions, which had itself been offered for sale by auction in 1903.

GREAT SNOW FALL
WAKEFIELD ROAD
HORBURY
XMAS 1906

72. Horbury Road at Christmas 1906. A great fall of snow has blocked the road, which is of course at this point largely free of houses, but it seems that either a tram or tram snow plough has got through.

73. William Walsham How, for long a country rector in Shropshire, had for some years been a suffragan bishop working in the East End of London before his appointment to Wakefield in 1888. Bishop How was both an able administrator and a beloved priest, and the news of his death in 1897 was received with real sadness in Wakefield, but he had come as bishop when in his mid-sixties, and he died at 73.

74. Albert Edward Sutcliffe Sugden was a professional teacher of music, and lived in Arundel Street. Here, he celebrates 21 years as choirmaster and organist at West Parade Wesleyan Methodist Chapel in Wakefield, in 1908. For a century and a half West Parade was the leading Methodist chapel in the town.

75. Charles George Milnes Gaskell, PC, MA, DL, died on 9 January 1919. He had had an active as well as a useful life: a barrister, he was an MP from 1885, Chairman of the West Riding County Council for 17 years from 1893, Chairman of the West Riding Rivers Board for a decade from 1893, a Privy Councillor from 1908. He was engaged in all good works locally, including involvement with local education and the foundation of the first park, as well as being the author of a number of books. In 1904 he was honoured with the degree of LLD by the nascent University of Leeds.

76. Joseph Barker, JP, a prominent participator in local well-doing in the later 19th century, was a subscriber of a substantial £500 to the creation of Clarence Park as Wakefield's first public park, opened in 1893. Major Barker owned the worsted spinning mills at Thornes, and after his purchase of the Holme Field estate in 1864 for £6,600, he considerably enlarged the house and arranged the estate in the 1860s and 1870s. He was a West Riding magistrate, a sometime Alderman of Wakefield, and major in the local Volunteers, an enthusiastic hunter with the Badsworth, a great supporter of Thornes Church; he was well-known as a reasonable, responsible millowner. He left a fortune of some £300,000 and the work people of his Thornes Mill erected this fountain in the new Public Park in his memory.

Grammar School, Wakefield.

77. The West Riding Proprietary School building of 1833/34, designed by Richard Lane of Manchester, survived in the hands of its originating company and providing liberal education for a couple of decades, until in 1854 it was purchased for a nominal sum and used to house Wakefield Grammar School. The photograph shows the building as it was in 1886, before additional building had been erected at either end of the original structure.

78. Young ladies at school: sports day, with parents and friends present in the grounds of the Girls' High School. Built in 1802/03 for John Pemberton Heywood, a Wakefield barrister and leading citizen, the house was bought by the Governors of the Grammar School in 1878 and for £8,000, to be opened in the same year as a Girls' High School.

79. A great fire at Silcoates School on 13 April 1904 destroyed a large part of what were then the more modern buildings, specifically built for the school and opened in 1893: the Georgian mansion at the centre of the estate did, however, survive. The school itself had been established in 1831 for the sons of Congregationalist ministers and missionaries, and after some initial difficulties, it became very successful, the sons of laymen being also admitted from the mid-1850s. New buildings, to replace those shown here burning, were opened in 1908.

80. Early Baden-Powell scouts: the organisation was established in 1908, and a group was obviously founded in connection with Holy Trinity Church, Wakefield.

Wakefield Asylum.

81. The West Riding was the first county to adopt the County Asylums Act of 1808, and in 1818 the West Riding Pauper Lunatic Asylum was opened in the outskirts of Wakefield, but in fact in the township of Stanley cum Wrenthorpe, in pleasant open countryside. It was later necessary to both extend the buildings in a major way, and to build two further large county asylums in the Riding.

82. A Dispensary for the benefit of the sick poor was founded in Wakefield in 1787, a hospital for the poor with infectious diseases in 1826, and an Eye Dispensary added in 1851. In 1854 Thomas Clayton (1786-1868), a wealthy and long-retired tallow chandler in the town, presented buildings to the Dispensary and ultimately left one half of his estate to the hospital. Despite the addition of further town-centre buildings, a larger site was felt necessary, and land was bought on the outskirts of the town at St. John's, where the foundation stone of the buildings shown in this photograph was laid in 1876, the plans being by William Bakewell (1839-1925), the Leeds architect. The road shown in front of the Clayton Hospital buildings was Victoria Square, part of a proposed housing development which never came about, and in later years the hospital premises were extended over it. The photograph shows the Milnes Gaskell extension at the rear of the right hand block, erected in 1897.

83. A convalescent home was established at Lupset Lodge for the benefit of women and children, in February 1888. It was entirely supported by subscriptions and by gifts in kind: Lady Catharine Milnes Gaskell of Thornes House was its president for many years and a major contributor to its well-being. The Home was still in existence in 1908.

Sandal Castle, Wakefield.

84. The ruins of Sandal Castle: a postcard used in 1914. After the despoilation of the Castle — and from 1645, its ruins seem to have appeared much as shewn here — although the site was privately owned, it seems to have been reasonably accessible to the public. It was formally leased to Wakefield Corporation in 1913 and bought by that body in 1954.

HOLMFIELD. THORNES PARK.

85. Holme Field − which incidentally was never in Thornes Park! − was a house the initial part of which was built in 1833 by Thomas Foljambe, a Wakefield lawyer and land speculator who was also clerk to the Barnsley Canal Co. In 1864 his heir sold Holme Field to Joseph Barker, a local worsted manufacturer, for £6,600, and he enlarged the house apparently twice before his death in 1892, when he left a fortune of over £300,000. In 1919 the house and estate were sold to Wakefield Corporation for £5,500.

86. Crazy Helen's Walk, Holme Field Park. This ancient way, the most direct route between Wakefield and Thornes before the opening of the Denby Dale Road under its Act of 1825, was later closed as a public footpath. Middle Stone Age flints have been found along the upper part of its route, and it may have been part of an ancient way which crossed the Calder towards the mesolithic flint site below Sandal Castle; its name could conceivably have some connection via popular myth, with Helen the mother of the Emperor Constantine: certain ancient routes in Wales were Sarn Helen. In more modern times, a poor mad woman was said to have lived in a hollow oak here.

Alverthorpe Hall, Wakefield.

87. Alverthorpe Hall was demolished in 1946. Built about 1700 (its first owner died in 1710), the house passed through many hands. Henry Clarkson, the author of delightful, published memories, lived there for several decades and died in 1896 at the age of 94, and the last of his (spinster) daughters in May 1921. The Hall was advertised for sale in 1921 and again in 1926, finding new owner/tenants on each occasion; during the Second World War it was occupied by the military. This postcard was used in 1907.

88. Thornes House was built in 1779-1781 for James Milnes, a wealthy Wakefield cloth merchant and sometime MP, to designs by John Carr, the great architect of York. It was occupied by Milnes and his relatives the Gaskells, until the death of C.G. Milnes Gaskell early in 1919, and in that year it was sold to Wakefield Corporation for £18,500; a secondary school was opened in the mansion in 1922.

THE LAKE. THORNES PARK. WAKEFIELD. 6.

89. The lake in Thornes Park. After the death of the Rt. Hon. Charles George Milnes Gaskell, barrister, politician, administrator, historian, in 1919, the Thornes House estate was sold to Wakefield Corporation, which initially intended to build council houses upon it. However, having bought the Snapethorpe Hall estate (which they proceeded to call Lupset), the Thornes estate was opened as a public park and the mansion itself utilised as a school. The fine landscaped parkland of Thornes was opened to the public in 1924, and included two lakes with a number of islands in them.

90. The Woolley Hall gardens, a card posted in 1908. The garden staff is shown together with greenhouses and flower beds, the garden being backed by a typically high and probably internally-flued wall.

91. Kettlethorpe Hall was built in 1727 for Gervase Norton, whose family had for long been settled on this estate. He chose an architecturally exuberant style, but dying without sons, his estate ultimately passed to his son-in-law and his daughter. From the latter lady it passed to her grandson and daughter, neither of whom married, but who left it to the Hon. G.C. Norton, whose only relationship to them seems to have been that he bore the same surname as that of their great-grandfather, Gervase Norton of Kettlethorpe. The house was let to a variety of tenants, all obviously of some financial standing, until in 1890 it was sold for £8,700 to the brothers T.K. and M.E. Sanderson, Wakefield corn merchants, the longer-lived of whom died in 1908, when the house was again sold, now to T.P. Tew of the Wakefield banking firm. In 1922 it was sold to J.H. Greaves of Wakefield, and in much later years to Wakefield Corporation, who opened there in 1952 their third Old People's Home. After a period of dereliction, the house is now undergoing restoration for domestic residential purposes.

92. The White House at Heath is believed to have been the last thatched property in the vicinity of Wakefield. The roof lines of numbers of older Wakefield properties suggest the widespread use of thatch in the town, but stone slates were in use by the 17th century, although thatch lingered in the rural areas around the town – in Normanton, for example well into the 19th century, and in the case of Heath, in this one instance, well into the 20th century.

93. Red Hall, Wakefield, was probably the first major building in the town and its vicinity to be built, about 1610, in red brick. It still exists in part. From the time of its purchase in the mid-seventeenth century until its being offered for sale by auction in 1896, Red Hall belonged to a family who came to build and live in Bramham Park.

94. After a prolonged gestation, and the purchase of a part of the site for the purpose more than two decades before its erection, Wakefield Town Hall was opened in 1880. The winner of a national competition for its design, T.E. Collcott of London, supervised the erection of the new Town Hall, whose foundation stone was laid by mayor Ald. W.H. Gill, solicitor, in October 1877. In this picture, mayor Ald. W.H. Lee, master worsted spinner, opens the new Town Hall in the presence of numerous other civic heads on October 1880.

95. The Coronation of Edward VII and Queen Alexandra in 1902 was the first coronation which there had been for over sixty years, and it was marked extensively. Here the ruins of Sandal Castle are surmounted by a pyre which was lit in June 1902.

96. The opening of a public memorial to Queen Victoria – who had died in 1901 – took place in the midst of an enormous crowd in February 1905, on the same day as the laying of the foundation stone of the Library in Drury Lane. The memorial was designed and executed by a Mr. Williamson of Esher in Surrey. Here, the Mayor of Wakefield, H.S. Childe, a mining engineer, with his wife, are in the presence of numerous mayors from neighbouring towns. The statue was removed from the Bull Ring to Denby Dale Road in 1950 and was returned to approximately its original site in 1985. In the rear of the picture is Union Street, which presumably derives its name from the Anglo-Irish Union of 1801, and gave its name to the Union Foundry there. Union Street was chosen as the site for an electricity sub-station in connection with the electric tramways whose wires and one of whose support posts may be seen.

97. The new king and queen, George V and Mary, during their visit to Wakefield and the industrial West Riding in July 1912: royal visits were in those days much less frequent. Here, the royal car passes the top of Market Street, amidst closely-pressing crowds. The huge Corn Exchange, which had been built during the 1830s, accommodates large numbers of onlookers: on the left is the shop of Harry Haley's athletic outfitters, marked by the bats, stumps and balls sign, then the entrance to the Grand Electric Cinema with its advertising boards, followed by one of Jeremiah Dunnill & Son's music shops (the other was at the end of Cheapside), followed by the offices of the Prudential Assurance Co. On the west side of Market Street — which led from the Corn Market to the Cattle Market — is one of the fine 18th century door cases to the Great Bull Inn, built early in the 1770s, and after the date of this photograph to be much altered in its ground floor elevation.

98. The chantry front at Kettlethorpe Hall park lake. The original front of the chantry chapel on Wakefield Bridge, a building which was licensed for public worship in 1356, was removed upon the rebuilding of the chapel in 1847/48 and rebuilt as an ornamental front to a small boathouse on the Kettlethorpe Hall estate, where it survives today, in municipal ownership. The Kettlethorpe housing estate now fills the fields which are to be seen in this photograph behind the stand of trees.

99. The interior of the church of Saint Mary on Wakefield Bridge. Entirely rebuilt in 1847/48, the church was then re-opened for public use. The chairs are doubtless somewhat later additions.

Trinity Church. Wakefield.

REV. E. T. ELLIOTT.

100. Trinity Church in George Street was built in 1838/39 and demolished in 1957, owing to an amalgamation of church livings. It was one of a number of in-town new churches of early Victorian times (of which only St. Andrew's survives), and its patronage was carefully kept out of the hands of the vicar of Wakefield. Curiously, the name of the minister shown was James Elliott, MA, Vicar of Holy Trinity from 1894 till 1904.

101. Westgate Chapel, the oldest place of worship in Wakefield after the cathedral, was opened in November 1752, to house a congregation which had been established in 1662. This photograph was taken before alterations made in the early 1880s. It shows not only the 18th century building and its fittings, including the two-decker pulpit, and the semi-circular singers' pew, but also the 19th century coloured windows (Wakefield-made in the early 1860s), and the monuments to Henry Briggs, the enlightened colliery owner, and Daniel Gaskell of Lupset Hall, Wakefield's first MP.

102. The Chantry Chapel on Wakefield Bridge, originally licensed for public worship in 1356 and used for that purpose until 1548, was entirely rebuilt from roadway level in 1847/48, and the new front then erected, and shown in this photograph, was itself replaced by the present front — the third — at the very beginning of the Second World War. This chantry on the bridge at Wakefield is one of only four which survive in England — the others are at Rotherham, St. Ives and Bradford on Avon. The building acted as a major support to the long and originally narrow bridge over the volatile River Calder. In the background on the right appear the two gables of the unusually-roofed buildings of the Stennard Works, built by Charles Clay for his agricultural implement manufactury in the early 1860s and later housing W.E. Garforth's Diamond Coal Cutter Company. On the left, the lower building is one of the 18th century waterside warehouses at the head of the Aire & Calder Navigation, which had its headquarters at Wakefield until 1851, and behind that the great railway corn warehouses at Kirkgate Station, operated by hydraulic power from an enginehouse whose chimney is probably that shown here.

103. The nave of Wakefield Cathedral is shown here with its (nearer) columnes of about 1150 and the further ones of about 1220, each interspersed with some later non-circular pillars. On the extreme right can be seen the doorway leading to the unusual room or parvise above the south porch which was itself for some time used to store the records of the Governors of the Wakefield Charities. The windows shown here are those 'restored' apparently in the 1880s, and they are filled with Victorian glass. The organ had been altered to this appearance in 1879.

104. Inside Wakefield Cathedral. This photograph looks from the nave into the chancel and shows the dividing screen of 1635 and above it on the left the stair-top doorway which led onto the medieval screen's top. The reredos shown here was given by a Col. Clapham of Manchester in 1896, and the photograph shows one of the 18th century chandeliers, one of which hung for some time in East Ardsley and later Wrenthorpe churches. The chancel was still the responsibility of, and insured by, the lay rectors, into at least the 1880s. An earlier bishop's throne is shown on the right of the chancel; the chancel itself was completely altered when the church was extended eastward as a memorial to the first bishop, the extension being consecrated in April 1905.

HOUSE OF MERCY, HORBURY.

105. The House of Mercy at Horbury was founded in 1858 by Reverend John Sharp, for long the incumbent of Horbury, to which living he had been presented by his father, the Vicar of Wakefield from 1810 to 1855. The foundation stones of purpose-built buildings were laid in 1862 and 1870, and numerous subsequent additions and alterations were made.

THE BISHOP'S PALACE, WAKEFIELD.

106. For some years after his appointment to the bishopric, William Walsham How occupied houses in and around Wakefield, but it was felt that an episcopal residence, specifically built, was desirable, although How was adamant that he did not wish to live in a palace. Land on the northern outskirts of Wakefield was acquired and in 1891 a contract was signed in the sum of £9,910 10s and the new house was occupied in 1893; the name Bishopgarth was chosen.

The Old Stocks, Kirkthorpe   Published by J. Ranns, Stationer, Wakefield. Valentines Series

107. Kirkthorpe and its stocks. A number of local villages retain the stonework of their stocks, where a culprit sat on a seat with his − or − her feet fastened ahead. The church had suffered a major restoration in 1851/52. The Cheesecake Inn stands between the stocks and the church.

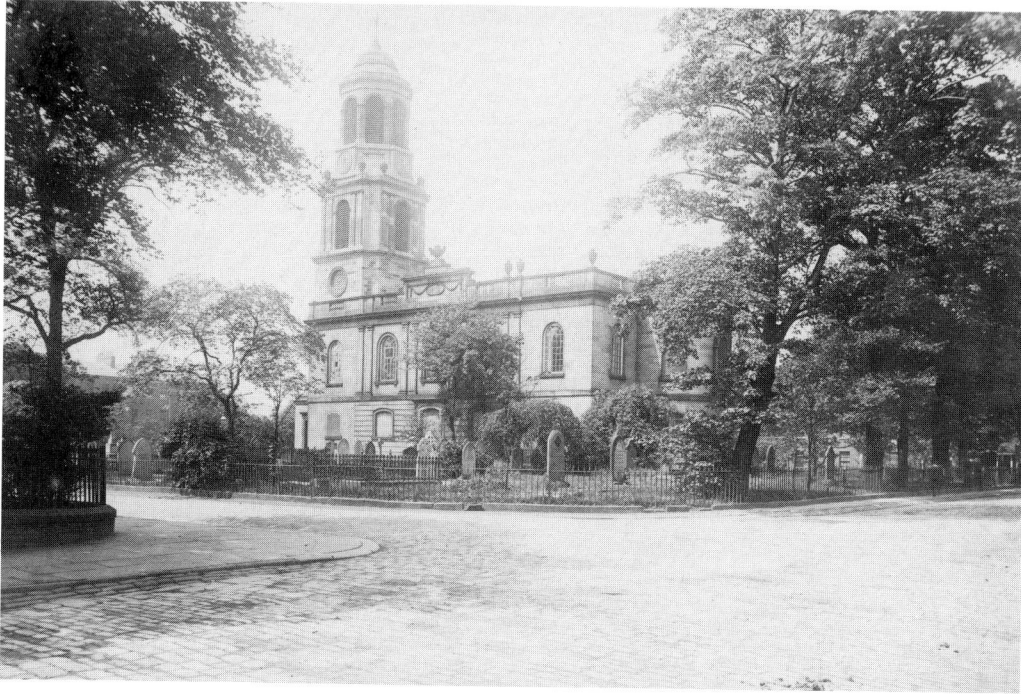

108. St. John's Church in calm Victorian sunshine. Consecrated in 1795, a major re-organisation had taken place in St. John's Church in the 1880s. The tower above the level of the nave roof was rebuilt in 1895, having for some years been reduced to the level of the nave. The semi-circular chancel which is shown here was rebuilt in 1904/05, and the infilling of the lower windows, shown here as accomplished, was undertaken as part of the 1880s restoration, when the side galleries, which of course had required light both below and above them, were removed. The church had been built as the centrepiece for a new town of Wakefield, developed by John Lee, the Wakefield attorney and land speculator, from 1791.